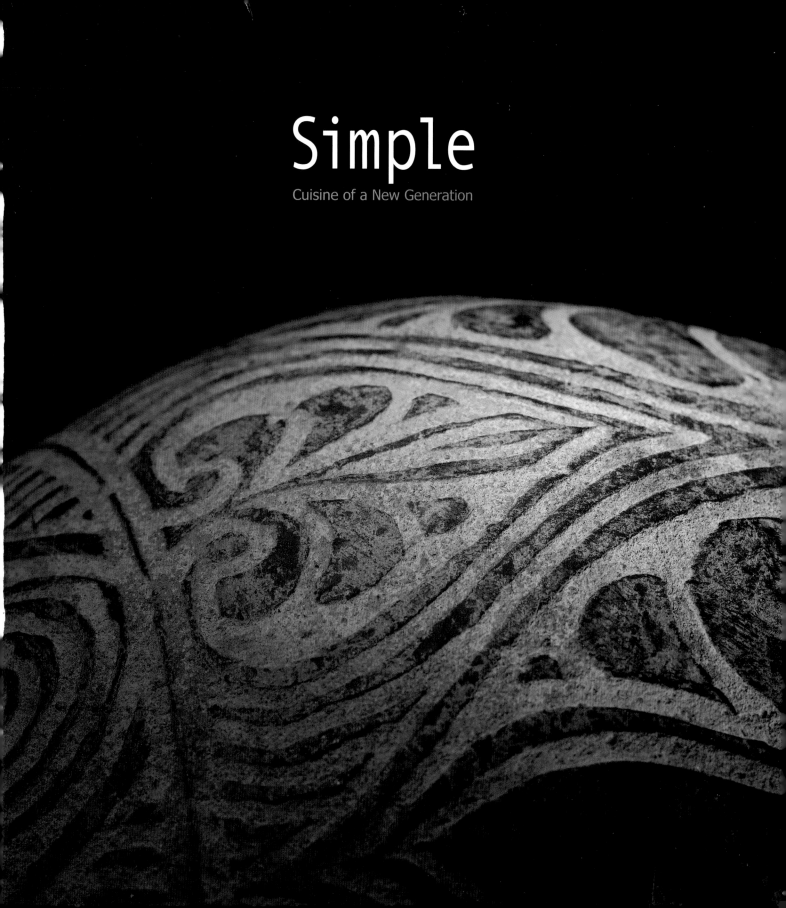

Simple

Cuisine of a New Generation

Simple

Cuisine of a New Generation

JIMMY
CHOK

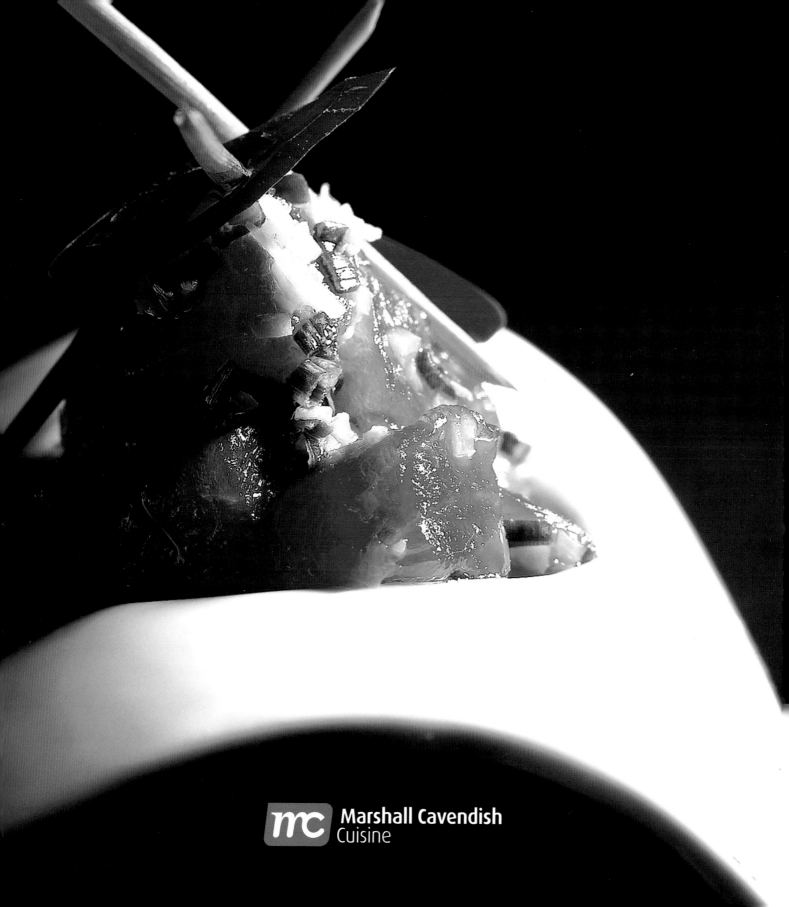

The Publisher wishes to thank **Sia Huat Pte Ltd** for the loan of their crockery and glassware.

Editor   : Lydia Leong
Designer   : Chris Wong
Photographer : Edmond Ho

Published by Marshall Cavendish Cuisine
An imprint of Marshall Cavendish International (Asia) Private Limited
A member of Times Publishing Limited
Times Centre, 1 New Industrial Road,
Singapore 536196
Tel: (65) 6213 9300   Fax: (65) 6285 4871
E-mail: te@sg.marshallcavendish.com
Online Bookstore:

http://www.marshallcavendish.com/genref

Malaysian Office:
Marshall Cavendish (Malaysia) Sdn Bhd (3024-D)
(General & Reference Publishing)
(Formerly known as Federal Publications Sdn Berhad)
Times Subang
Lot 46, Persiaran Teknologi Subang
Subang Hi-Tech Industrial Park
Batu Tiga, 40000 Shah Alam
Selangor Darul Ehsan, Malaysia
Tel: (603) 5635 2191, 5628 6888
Fax: (603) 5635 2706
E-mail: cchong@my.marshallcavendish.com

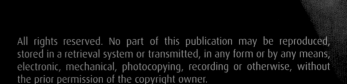

National Library Board Singapore Cataloguing in Publication Data

Chok, Jimmy, 1970-
Simple : cuisine of a new generation / Jimmy Chok. – Singapore :
Marshall Cavendish Cuisine, c2005.
p. cm.

ISBN : 981-232-936-6

1.   Cookery, Asian. I. Title.

TX724.5.A1
641.595 -- dc21   SLS2005018866

Printed in Singapore by Tien Wah Press Pte Ltd

To Jennifer, Javan and
Joey for your love and
encouragement.
To mum and dad for your
love and continuous support
for my choice of career.

AMUSE BUSCHE

25 Baked Wakame Tart with Seared Scallop

26 Button Mushrooms Sautéed with Balsamic Vinegar

31 Chilled Bean Curd with Caviar

32 Chilled Pea Soup with Poached Tiger Prawn

36 Solf-boiled Quail's Egg with Tobiko

38 Raw Tuna with Pickled Ginger and Spring Onion Oil

40 Cucumber Jelly with Lemon Segment

42 Shiitake Mushroom Mousse with Truffle Oil

44 Skewered Cherry Tomato, Mozarella and Basil

46 Smoked Salmon Cucumber Roll with Garam Marsala Cream

APPETISERS

50   Cold Marinated Angel Hair Pasta with Sliced Australia Abalone

52   Crab Cakes with Tomato Jam

54   Deep-fried Soft Shell Crab with Wasabi Tobiko
and Lime Beurre Blanc

56   Foie Gras Burger

58   Grilled Jumbo Prawns with Pineapple Cucumber Salad
and Lime Cincaluk Dressing

63   Grilled Lemon Grass Skewered Tiger Prawns with
Capsicum Chilli Chutney

64   Hot Seared Salmon Fillet with Ginger, Lime, Chilli
and Sweet Soy Sauce Dressing

66   Hot Seared Scallop with Chuka Kurage
and Sesame Thai Chilli Dressing

68   Lightly Marinated Fennel Salad with Salmon Roe,
Pomegranate Seeds and Blood Orange Sorbet

70   Maguro Loin Wrapped in Nori and Bean Curd Skin
with Avocado Salsa, Wasabi Mayonnaise and Soy Mirin Glaze

72   Pan-fried Foie Gras with Braised Red Cabbage
and Mushroom Dumpling

74   Prawn and Scallop Ravioli with Kaffir Lime Beurre Blanc

76   Roast Duck Mango Rice Paper Roll
with Spiced Mango Chutney

81   Silken Bean Curd and Roma Tomato Salad with
Chinese Black Vinegar Reduction and Sichuan Pepper Salt

82   Steamed Silken Bean Curd with Wood Ear
and Black Vinegar Sauce

84   Wok-fried Sliced Beef with Ulam Greens
and Lime Chilli Bean Dressing

SOUPS

88   Cappuccino of Green Pea with Seared Scallop
and Ham and Pea Salad

90   Fresh Salmon and Bean Curd with Bonito Miso Broth

93   Roast Duck Broth with Duck Liver Dumplings and Baby Spinach

96   Roasted Pumpkin Soup with Sautéed Slipper Lobster,
Milk Foam and White Truffle Oil

98   Silk Hen Chinese Herb Broth with Mushroom Ravioli
and Chinese Wolfberries

MAIN COURSES

102 Baked Soy Chilean Sea Bass with Edamame Beans,
Semi-dried Tomatoes and Soy Mirin Glaze

104 Braised Lamb Shank with Oyster Sauce, Chinese Wine
and Red Dates

106 Braised Pork Belly with Grilled Portobello, Poached Egg
and Pickled Ginger Mayonnaise

108 Braised Oxtail and Cèpes Mushroom in Phyllo Pastry

110 Confit of Miso Sake Veal Cheek with Asian Spice Couscous

115 Asian Spice Confit of Duck Leg with Sichuan Pepper Chilli
and Salt Dust

116 Coriander Crusted Rack of Lamb with Baby
Chinese White Cabbage and Orange Hoisin Sauce

118 Dark Soy Sauce Quail with Poached Quail's Egg
and Chinese Kale

120 Five-spice Duck Breast with Sautéed Spiced Potatoes
and Sweet Plum Sauce

122 Pan-fried Halibut Fillet with Sweet Pea and New Potato Salad
and Grain Mustard Dressing

124 Pan-fried Sea Bass Fillet with Pickled Ginger Red Wine
Butter Sauce

126 Pan-fried Sea Bream Fillet with Baby Bitter Gourd Salad

128 Baked Red Mullet with Tomato Lemon Salsa

130 Roasted Lamb Rump with Sautéed Japanese Mushrooms
and Fermented Black Bean Sauce

132 Roasted Veal Tenderloin with Sautéed Mushrooms
and Curry Leaf-infused Black Pepper Sauce

135 Seared Tuna Steak with Miso Mustard Sabayon
and White Radish Ginger Coulis

136 Slow-cooked Salmon Fillet with Simple Fennel Salad
and Goma Konbu

138 Steamed Maine Lobster with Wakame in Hot Garlic Oil

142 Steamed Threadfin Belly with Sweet Mui Choi Crust
and Sautéed Chinese Leek

144 Stir-fried Linguini with Garlic, Chilli, Mushrooms, Spinach
and Spring Onion

DESSERTS

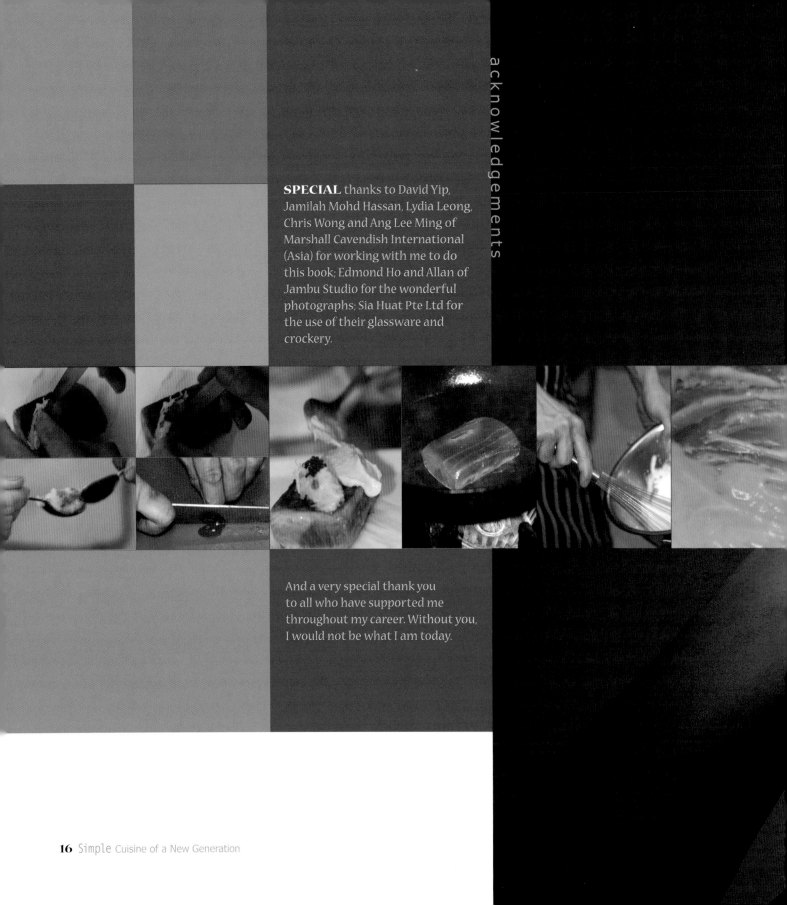

acknowledgements

SPECIAL thanks to David Yip, Jamilah Mohd Hassan, Lydia Leong, Chris Wong and Ang Lee Ming of Marshall Cavendish International (Asia) for working with me to do this book; Edmond Ho and Allan of Jambu Studio for the wonderful photographs; Sia Huat Pte Ltd for the use of their glassware and crockery.

And a very special thank you to all who have supported me throughout my career. Without you, I would not be what I am today.

JIMMY Chok's life is a success story that many chefs can only aspire to. What he has managed to accomplish since beginning his culinary career has made him an inspiration to those in the food and beverage industry, although those who know him will recognise that it has not come without much sweat and tears.

When he first started out at Raffles Hotel, he had no formal training as a chef and no understanding of what he was getting into. But over the years, through hard work and dedication, he has really proved capable and I was delighted to watch him come of age, as it were, with his latest restaurant venture. He is both the executive chef and the sole proprietor of the establishment called Salt, and was one of the first few chefs in Singapore to openly embrace fusion cooking. By doing so, he demonstrated a degree of tenacity that was highly unusual for chefs of his generation. He found something he was good at and made no apologies for it, on top of which he was handpicked as a contributor to a collaborative fusion cookbook called "Crossroads" in 2001. He has also been recognised by the media and in various culinary competitions of the highest calibre, such as the Bocuse d'Or National Selection in Singapore.

One of Jimmy's strengths is his innate sense of style, with his smart-casual demeanor and distinctive approach to food presentation—polished, charming, and bold. You'll see examples of it in this book. He has even added a little suspense by publishing recipes that leave something to the imagination of the reader. No doubt, he will continue to take up new culinary ventures, such as this first personal cookbook of his, in order to keep his ideas fresh and his cooking youthful.

Congratulations Jimmy, on another milestone in your career.

Peter A Knipp
Managing Director, PKH
Co-organiser, World Gourmet Summit, Singapore

BEING self-taught, I faced many difficulties when I first started out in my career. But through it all, I have learnt much and this book is my interpretation of cooking.

I believe cooking doesn't always need to elaborate in order to be the best or to achieve the best results. I have realised that sometimes keeping things simple is more difficult to achieve. Using the choicest and freshest produce or ingredients can make the difference in the final dish. Many of these recipes take just four to five steps to do and the ingredients are readily available from the market or supermarket.

Many ingredients used in these recipes are my personal favourites. They include hoisin sauce, sweet dark soy sauce (*kicap manis*), limes and Chinese wine. Having lived in Singapore and Malaysia, these ingredients are what I grew up with and using them comes naturally to me.

In order for readers to have a free rein on the final presentation of the dishes, I have chosen to leave garnishes and side dishes out of

some of the recipes. Readers can then add their own touches to the recipes to make them their own. As such, the recipes in this book are not meant to be followed by rote. They can be adapted to taste and the ingredients can be substituted according to personal preference.

In essence, cooking should be simple and enjoyable. It is with these thoughts in mind that I have written these recipes.

Jimmy Chok
June 2005

AMUSE BUSCHE

Baked **Wakame Tart** with Seared Scallop

Ingredients

Puff pastry	1 small circle, 2.5-cm in diameter
Wakame	2 g
Scallop	1
Salt	to taste
Ground black pepper	to taste
Shichimi togarashi	a pinch
Cooking oil	a dash
Olive oil	a dash
Light soy sauce	a dash

Method

⊙ Bake puff pastry in an oven at 180°C for about 4 minutes. Remove and top with wakame.

⊙ Return to oven and bake further until pastry is cooked.

⊙ Season scallop with salt, pepper and *shichimi togarashi*. Heat cooking oil and sear scallop over high heat.

⊙ Place scallop on pastry. Drizzle with dash of olive oil and light soy sauce before serving.

Note

Bake the pastry before topping with the wakame, as the flavour of the seaweed is easily destroyed by overcooking.

Prepare the scallop only after the pastry is ready as it may dry out if cooked too early.

Button Mushrooms
Sautéed with Balsamic Vinegar

Ingredients

Red onion	5 g, peeled and chopped
Olive oil	10 ml
Fresh button mushrooms	2
Balsamic vinegar	a dash
Chopped spring onion (scallion)	

Method

- Heat olive oil and sweat onion.
- Add mushrooms and cook for about 2 minutes then deglaze with balsamic vinegar.
- Garnish with spring onion and serve.

Note

Allow the mushrooms to sit for a little while after cooking to absorb the flavour of the balsamic vinegar.

Chilled Bean Curd with Caviar

Ingredients

Bean curd	10 g, chilled
Caviar	1 tsp
Olive oil	a dash
Chives	

Method

- Cut bean curd to the desired shape. Top with caviar and drizzle with a dash of olive oil.
- Garnish with chives and serve.

Note

This recipe is very simple, but the flavours of the caviar and bean curd are well-matched.

Chilled Pea Soup with Poached Tiger Prawn

Ingredients

Green peas	100 g
Sweet pea pod	1
Tiger prawn (shrimp)	1, peeled, leaving tail on and cooked
Salt	to taste
Ground black pepper	to taste

Method

- Blanch green peas with hot water and then soak in cold water to cool.
- Blend (process) cooled peas with 100 ml cold water and chill.
- Split pea pod and place tiger prawn in it.
- Serve chilled soup in a glass and arrange prawn in pea pod on rim of glass.

Note

Blanching the green peas helps to cook them and remove any bitterness in taste.

Soaking the green peas in cold water after blanching will stop the cooking process and prevent the peas from overcooking.

Soft-boiled **Quail's Egg** with Tobiko

Ingredients

Quail's egg	1
Salt	to taste
Ground black pepper	to taste
Tobiko	½ tsp
Chervil	

Method

⊙ Place egg in boiling water and cook for about 3 minutes. Remove and leave to cool in ice water.

⊙ Peel egg and cut in half. The egg yolk should still be slightly runny. Season with salt and pepper.

⊙ Top egg halves with *tobiko* and chervil. Serve immediately at room temperature.

Raw Tuna with Pickled Ginger and Spring Onion Oil

Ingredients

Pickled ginger	10 g, chopped
Spring onion (scallion)	10 g, chopped
Olive oil	20 ml
Raw tuna	30 g
Light soy sauce	a dash
Red chilli slices	
Chives	
Shimichi togarashi	a pinch

Method

⊙ Mix ginger, spring onion and olive oil together.

⊙ Cut tuna into small cubes and place on a small plate.

⊙ Spoon olive oil mixture over tuna and drizzle with dash of light soy sauce.

⊙ Garnish with red chilli slices and chives. Serve with a pinch of shimichi togarashi.

Note

Use only very fresh tuna for this recipe.

Humidity destroys the flavour and freshness of tuna very easily. Thus, cut the tuna just before serving.

Cucumber Jelly with Lemon Segment

Ingredients

Cucumber	1
Water	50 ml
Gelatine powder	1 tsp
Salt	to taste
Ground black pepper	to taste
Lemon segments	
Grated lemon rind	
Chervil	

Method

- Cut, then blend cucumber with water and strain. Discard residue and reserve liquid.

- Dilute gelatine power with some warm water then mix into strained cucumber liquid. Season with salt and pepper and pour into a glass. Allow to set in the refrigerator.

- Top jelly with lemon segments and grated lemon rind. Garnish with chervil.

Note

The cucumber jelly can be prepared a day in advance and kept refrigerated before serving.

Shiitake Mushroom Mousse
with Truffle Oil

Ingredients

Olive oil	5 ml
Red onion	10 g, peeled and chopped
Fresh shiitake mushrooms	50 g
White wine	10 ml
Canned chicken stock	20 ml
Cream	50 ml
Salt	to taste
Ground black pepper	to taste
Truffle oil	a dash

Method

- Heat olive oil and sweat onion. Add mushrooms and deglaze with wine.
- Add chicken stock and cook until mushrooms are soft before adding a little cream. Season to taste with salt and pepper.
- Blend (process) mushroom mixture into a purée. Leave to cool.
- Whip remaining cream and add to purée. Allow mousse to set in the refrigerator.
- Quenelle mousse onto a dish or spoon. Drizzle with a dash of truffle oil and garnish as desired before serving.

Note

Allow the purée to cool down before folding in the whipped cream to prevent the cream from melting.

Skewered **Cherry Tomato**, Mozarella and Basil

Ingredients

Cherry tomato	1, cut in half
Mozzarella	5 g, cut into 2 triangles
Basil leaf	1
Olive oil	a dash
Balsamic reduction*	a dash
Flake salt	a pinch
Freshly cracked black pepper	a pinch
Bamboo skewer	1

Method

- Skewer tomato halves and mozzarella triangles with bamboo skewer and place on basil leaf.
- Drizzle with olive oil and balsamic reduction.
- Sprinkle with salt and pepper before serving.

*Balsamic Reduction

Ingredients

Balsamic vinegar	100 ml
Sugar	20 g

Method

- Bring vinegar and sugar to the boil, then simmer over low heat until reduced to a third. Store in a clean bottle and use as needed.

Smoked Salmon
Cucumber Roll with Garam Marsala Cream

Ingredients

Cucumber	10 g, julienned
Smoked salmon slice	30 g
Garam marsala	a pinch
Whipped cream	5 g

Method

- Place julienned cucumber on smoked salmon slice and roll up. Cut into halves.
- Mix garam marsala with whipped cream and spoon over salmon roll before serving.

Note

This simple recipe can be prepared ahead of time and kept refrigerated until needed.

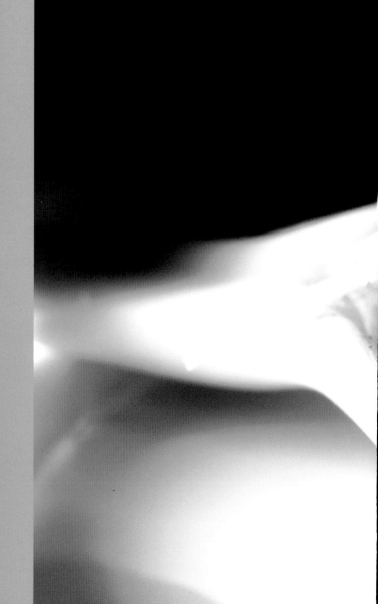

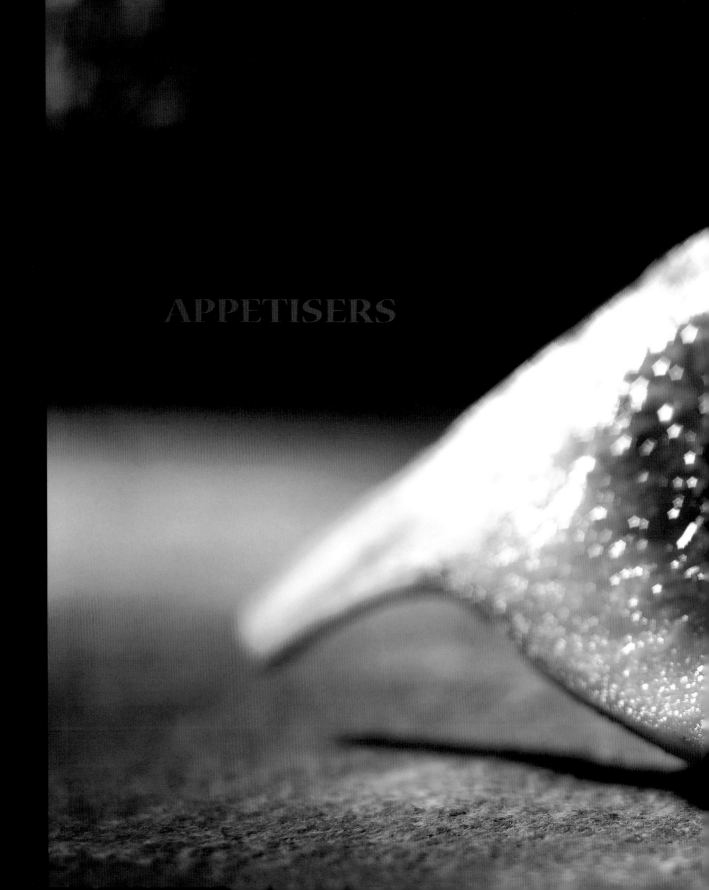

APPETISERS

Cold Marinated Angel Hair Pasta with
Sliced Australia Abalone

Ingredients

Angel hair pasta	100 g, cooked in salted water
Canola oil	10 ml
Japanese mayonnaise	10 g
Mirin	20 ml
Salt	to taste
Ground black pepper	to taste
Tobiko	20 g
Canned Australian abalone	80 g, sliced
Daikon cress	
Chopped spring onion (scallion)	

Method

- Marinate cooked angel hair pasta with canola oil, mayonnaise and mirin.
- Season to taste with salt and pepper, then mix in *tobiko*.
- Arrange on plate with sliced abalone. Garnish with daikon cress and spring onion to serve.

Note

Marinate the pasta one day ahead for the flavours to be fully absorbed.

When cooking the pasta, cook it for a while longer after it reaches the al dente stage, so it will remain tender when cold.

Crab Cakes with Tomato Jam

Ingredients

Salt	to taste
Ground black pepper	to taste
Plain (all-purpose) flour for coating	
Egg	1, beaten
Breadcrumbs for coating	
Cooking oil for deep-frying	

Crab Patties

Crab meat	120 g
Red, yellow and green capsicums (bell peppers)	50 g, finely diced
Red onion	10 g, peeled and finely chopped
Spring onion (scallion)	1, finely chopped
Kaffir lime leaf	1, finely chopped
Cumin seeds	8, finely ground
Coriander (cilantro) leaves	1 sprig, finely chopped
Eggs	1
Breadcrumbs	20 g
Mayonnaise	10 g
Mustard	5 g

Tomato Jam

Ripe tomatoes	200 g, chopped
Red onions	50 g, peeled and chopped
Garlic	5 cloves
Red chillies	2
Canola oil	80 ml
Honey	30 ml

Method

- Combine ingredients for crab patties and season to taste with salt and pepper.
- Divide mixture into 3 portions and shape each into a patty. Freeze for 2 hours.
- Run patties through flour, then coat with beaten egg and breadcrumbs.
- Deep-fry until golden brown.
- Blend (process) tomato jam ingredients together and bring to the boil over low heat, stirring constantly, until mixture becomes thick and jam-like.
- Serve crab cakes with tomato jam and a vegetable salad of your choice.

Note

Ripe tomatoes will give the tomato jam a better flavour and sweetness.

The frozen crab cakes need not be thawed before deep-frying.

Deep-fried **Soft Shell Crab** with Wasabi Tobiko and Lime Beurre Blanc

Ingredients

Soft shell crab	1
Salt	to taste
Ground black pepper	to taste
Corn flour (cornstarch)	20 g
Cooking oil for deep-frying	
Cucumber	50 g, julienned
Cherry tomatoes	3, each cut in half

Lime Beurre Blanc

White wine	50 ml
Onion	10 g, peeled and sliced
Cream	30 ml
Butter	50 g
Limes	2, grated for zest and squeezed for juice
Sugar	to taste
Wasabi *tobiko*	10 g

Method

- Season crab with salt and pepper then coat with corn flour.

- Heat oil and deep-fry crab. Drain and set aside.

- Prepare lime beurre blanc. Bring wine to the boil and add onion. Allow to boil until reduced by half, then stir in cream.

- Return to the boil, then whisk in butter. Season with lime zest and juice and sugar. Add wasabi *tobiko* when ready to serve.

- Arrange cucumber, cherry tomatoes and fried crab on a plate. Spoon sauce around before serving.

Note

When defrosting soft shell crab, leave it flat on a plate in the refrigerator. Avoid handling it too much as it is very fragile. The claws and legs break very easily.

Foie gras	100 g
Salt	to taste
Ground black pepper	to taste
Nameko mushrooms	20 g
Butter	20 g
Red onions	30 g, peeled and sliced
Sugar	to taste
Chinese steamed bun (*mantou*)	1, deep-fried until golden brown then cut in half
Arugula (rocket salad)	20 g

Sauce

Port	20 ml
Red wine	20 ml
Canned chicken stock	80 ml
Chinese wolfberries	5 g
Butter	10 g

- Season foie gras with salt and pepper to taste. Pan-fry over high heat and set aside.

- Quickly sauté mushrooms over high heat with butter. Set aside.

- In the same pan, sauté onions with a little sugar until caramalised. Set aside.

- Prepare sauce. Combine port and red wine and bring to the boil until reduced by half. Add chicken stock and wolfberries. Reduce further by half and whisk in butter.

- Place one half of bun on a plate, then top with foie grass and arugula.

- Spoon sautéed mushrooms and caramalised onions on top, then sandwich with other half of bun. Drizzle sauce around before serving.

Note

Deep-fry the Chinese steamed bun only when ready to serve, as it will turn hard when cooled

Grilled **Jumbo Prawns** with Pineapple
Cucumber Salad and Lime Cincaluk Dressing

Ingredients

Jumbo prawns (shrimps)	3, butterflied with shell on
Salt	to taste
Ground black pepper	to taste

Pineapple Cucumber Salad

Pineapple	100 g, sliced
Cucumber	80 g, sliced and seeded
Red onions	30 g, peeled and sliced
Red chilli	1, sliced
Sugar	to taste
Limes	2, squeezed for juice

Lime *Cincaluk* Dressing

Limes	4, grated for zest and squeezed for juice
Red chilli	1, sliced
Fermented prawn (shrimp) paste (*cincaluk*)	30 ml
Red onions	30 g, peeled and sliced
Sugar	20 g
Olive oil	10 ml
Kaffir lime leaf	1, finely sliced

Method

- Season prawns with salt and pepper and grill to cook.
- Mix salad ingredients together.
- Mix dressing ingredients together.
- Arrange salad on a plate with grilled prawns. Spoon dressing over before serving.

Note

To butterfly prawns, make a slit along the length of the prawns from the head down to the back.

The dressing can be prepared a day ahead and refrigerated. This will allow it to mature and have a better flavour.

Grilled Lemon Grass Skewered **Tiger Prawns**
with Capsicum Chilli Chutney

Ingredients

Tiger prawns (shrimps)	3, each about 20 g, peeled, leaving tails intact
Salt	to taste
Ground black pepper	to taste
Lemon grass	1 stalk, outer leaves discarded and tip cut to create a sharp point

Capsicum Chilli Chutney

Red capsicums (bell peppers)	200 g, diced
Red onions	20 g, peeled and diced
Canola oil	15 ml
Red chillies	20 g, seeded and diced
Sugar	50 g
Red wine vinegar	80 ml

Method

- Season prawns with salt and pepper, then skewer using lemon grass. Set aside.
- Grill bell peppers over an open flame until skins turn black. Peel off burnt skins. Discard seeds and dice.
- Sweat red onions with canola oil until soft.
- Add capsicums, chilli, sugar and vinegar and cook over low heat, stirring constantly, until mixture is thick.
- Grill prawns and serve with chutney.

Note

The chutney can be prepared ahead of time, as it will take a while for it to thicken. Stir constantly to prevent it from burning.

Hot **Seared Salmon Fillet** with Ginger, Lime, Chilli and Sweet Soy Sauce Dressing

Ingredients

Salmon fillet	3 slices, each about 30 g
Salt	to taste
Ground black pepper	to taste
Cooking oil	a dash
Coriander (cilantro) leaves	
Chives	
Cherry tomato	1, cut in half

Sweet Soy Sauce Dressing

Ginger	10 g, peeled and chopped
Lime	2, grated for zest and squeezed for juice
Red chilli	1, chopped and seeded
Red onions	20 g, peeled and chopped
Indonesian sweet soy sauce	100 ml
Spring onion (scallion)	1, chopped

Method

⊙ Season salmon with salt and pepper to taste. Heat oil and sear salmon over high heat until just done. Dish out.

⊙ Combine dressing ingredients and spoon over salmon.

⊙ Garnish with coriander, chives and cherry tomato to serve.

Note

Be careful not to overcook salmon as the meat will become very dry.

Alternatively, sear a larger piece of salmon, then slice it to serve.

Hot Seared Scallop with Chuka Kurage and
Sesame Thai Chilli Dressing

Ingredients

Scallops	3, large
Salt	to taste
Ground black pepper	to taste
Cooking oil	a dash
Chuka kurage (marinated jellyfish)	80 g
Daikon cress	

Sesame Thai Chilli Dressing

Thai chilli sauce	100 ml
White sesame seeds	2 g, dry-roasted
Limes	2, grated for zest and squeezed for juice
Red onion	10 g, peeled and chopped
Spring onion (scallion)	1, chopped
Sesame oil	a dash

Method

⊙ Season scallops with salt and pepper. Heat oil and sear over high heat.

⊙ Combine chilli dressing ingredients.

⊙ Arrange *chuka kurage* on a plate with scallops. Spoon dressing around. Garnish with daikon cress or as desired before serving.

Note

There are many brands of Thai chilli sauce available and they all have different levels of sweetness and sourness. Adjust the taste of the dressing according to your preference.

Lightly **Marinated Fennel Salad** with
Salmon Roe, Pomegranate Seeds and Blood Orange Sorbet

Ingredients

Fennel	100 g, thinly sliced
Lemon	1, grated for zest and squeezed for juice
Sugar	to taste
Salt	to taste
Ground black pepper	to taste
Salmon roe	5 g
Pomegranate seeds	20 g
Parsley	
Blood orange or other citrus-based sorbet	1 scoop
Olive oil	a dash

Method

⊙ Soak sliced fennel in ice water for about 10 minutes to allow it to become crisp.

⊙ Drain fennel and marinate with lemon zest and juice, sugar, salt and pepper.

⊙ Arrange on a plate and sprinkle salmon roe, pomegranate seeds and parsley around.

⊙ Top with a scoop of sorbet and drizzle with olive oil before serving.

Maguro Loin Wrapped in Nori and
Bean Curd Skin with Avocado Salsa, Wasabi Mayonnaise and Soy Mirin Glaze

Ingredients

Maguro loin (tuna)	100 g
Nori	1 sheet
Dried bean curd skin	1 sheet, soaked in water
Olive oil	20 ml
Avocado	1, peeled and chopped
Japanese mayonnaise	10 ml
Sugar	to taste
Lemon	1, squeezed for juice
Salt	to taste
Ground black pepper	to taste
Mirin	20 ml
Light soy sauce	20 ml
Corn flour (cornstarch)	5 g
Goma wakame	50 g
Tobiko	30 g
Wasabi	10 ml
Mayonnaise	20 ml

Method

⊙ Wrap *maguro* loin with nori, then wrap again with bean curd skin. Roll up tightly.

⊙ Pan-fry over low heat with olive oil until golden brown. Slice and set aside.

⊙ Mix avocado with Japanese mayonnaise, then season with sugar, lemon juice, salt and pepper. Set aside.

⊙ Bring mirin and light soy sauce to the boil and thicken with corn flour. Remove from heat and set aside.

⊙ Arrange wakame on a plate with roll. Serve with avocado, *tobiko*, wasabi, mayonnaise and mirin and light soy sauce glaze.

Note

Mix the avocado and Japanese mayonnaise at the time of serving to avoid it from turning black.

To give more flavour to the *maguro*, use a little soy glaze to marinate it before wrapping.

Pan-fried Foie Gras with
Braised Red Cabbage and Mushroom Dumpling

Ingredients

Foie gras	100 g
Cooking oil	30 ml
Red onions	30 g, peeled and sliced
Red cabbage	200 g
Red wine	100 ml
Red wine vinegar	100 ml
Bay leaves	2
Sugar	80 g
Salt	to taste
Ground black pepper	to taste
Wonton skin	1, round

Mushroom Ragout

Butter	20 g
Red onions	20 g, peeled and chopped
Fresh shiitake mushrooms	20 g, chopped
Fresh button mushrooms	20 g, chopped
Oyster mushrooms	20 g, chopped
Cream	50 ml
Spring onions (scallions)	10 g, chopped
Salt	to taste
Ground black pepper	to taste

Method

- Sear foie gras over high heat to get a crisp skin. Set aside.
- Heat oil and sweat onions. Add cabbage, then deglaze with wine and vinegar.
- Add bay leaves and sugar, and cook until liquid dries completely. Season with salt and pepper.
- Prepare mushroom ragout. Heat butter and sweat onions.
- Add mushrooms and stir in cream and spring onions. Season with salt and pepper. Cook until ragout thickens.
- Spoon ragout onto wonton skin and fold into a parcel. Steam for 5 minutes.
- Arrange cabbage on a plate and top with foie gras and dumpling. Garnish as desired before serving.

Note

Steam the dumpling only when you are ready to serve it. This will prevent the skin from separating from the ragout when it cools.

Prawn and **Scallop Ravioli** with
Kaffir Lime Beurre Blanc

Ingredients

Salt	to taste
Ground black pepper	to taste
Wonton skins	3, round

Ravioli Filling

Scallops	20 g, chopped
Prawns (shrimps)	20 g, peeled and chopped
Red onion	5 g, peeled and chopped
Coriander (cilantro) leaves	2 g, choped
Spring onion (scallion)	2 g, chopped
Red chilli	2 g, chopped
Light soy sauce	5 ml

Kaffir Lime Beurre Blanc

White wine	50 ml
Red onion	10 g, peeled and chopped
Cream	20 ml
Butter	80 g
Kaffir lime leaf	1, finely sliced
Kaffir limes	2, grated for zest
Lime	1, squeezed for juice
Salt	to taste
Ground black pepper	to taste

Method

- Mix ravioli filling ingredients together and season with salt and pepper.
- Divide into 3 even portions and spoon onto wonton skins. Fold wonton skins over to enclose filling.
- Poach ravioli for about 6 minutes in simmering salted water.
- Prepare kaffir lime beurre blanc. Bring wine to the boil and add onion. Allow it to reduce before stirring in cream and whisking in butter.
- Add kaffir lime leaf and zest and lime juice. Season to taste with salt and pepper.
- Spoon kaffir lime beurre blanc over ravioli before serving.

Note

Ravioli can be made ahead of time and kept in the freezer.

Roast Duck and Mango Rice Paper Roll
with Spiced Mango Chutney

Ingredients

Vietnamese rice paper	1 sheet
Roast duck meat	120 g, julienned
Carrot	20 g, julienned
Cucumber	20 g, jullienned
Spring onion (scallion)	1, julienned
Coriander (cilantro) leaves	1 sprig
Ripe Thai mango	40 g, peeled and julienned

Spiced Mango Chutney

Semi-ripe Thai mango	150 g, peeled and julienned
Mustard seeds	2 g
Mango powder	5 g
Sugar	30 g
Vinegar	50 ml
Red onions	20 g, peeled and julienned
Canola oil	50 ml

Method

- Combine mango chutney ingredients and cook until thick.
- Soak rice paper in warm water, then remove and place on a damp towel.
- Place duck meat, carrot, cucumber, spring onion, coriander and mango on one edge of rice paper and roll up.
- Cut rice paper roll in half and serve with mango chutney.

Note

Prepare all the filling ingredients before preparing the rice paper, since the rice paper dries up very quickly.

Silken Bean Curd and Roma Tomato Salad with
Chinese Black Vinegar Reduction and Sichuan Pepper Salt

Ingredients

Silken bean curd (round)	80 g, sliced
Roma tomato	1, sliced
Basil leaves	20 g
Black vinegar	100 ml
Sugar	50 g
Sichuan peppercorns	10, dry-roasted
Flake salt	a pinch
Olive oil	a dash

Method

⊚ Arrange bean curd, tomato and basil on a plate.

⊚ Heat vinegar and sugar and reduce by a third over low heat.

⊚ Grind Sichuan peppercorns and mix with salt.

⊚ Sprinkle Sichuan pepper salt over bean curd, tomato and basil. Serve with a drizzle of vinegar reduction and a dash of olive oil.

Note

Toast the peppercorns over moderate heat, since high heat will give them a bitter taste.

Steamed **Silken Bean Curd** with
Wood Ear and Black Vinegar Sauce

Ingredients

Silken bean curd (round)	1, cut into slices
Cooking oil	a dash
Red onions	20 g, peeled and sliced
Garlic	3 cloves, peeled and finely chopped
Ginger	20 g, peeled and sliced
Black vinegar	100 ml
Sugar	to taste
Wood ear fungus	30 g, soaked, drained and sliced
Coriander (cilantro) leaves	

Method

- Steam bean curd for about 6 minutes.

- Heat oil and sweat onions, garlic and ginger until soft.

- Add vinegar and bring to the boil. Season with sugar to taste.

- Add wood ear fungus and bring to the boil for about 5 minutes.

- Spoon sauce over bean curd and garnish with coriander.

Note

When buying wood ear fungus, choose the larger pieces as small ones have a tougher root base.

As a variation to this recipe, use ready-to-eat bean curd and serve cold.

Wok-fried Sliced Beef with Ulam Greens
and Lime Chilli Bean Dressing

Ingredients

Topside beef	120 g, thinly sliced
Salt	to taste
Ground black pepper	to taste
Cooking oil	a dash
Red onions	30 g, peeled and sliced
Chilli bean sauce	30 ml
Oyster sauce	10 ml
Lime	3, grated for zest and squeezed for juice
Sugar	10 g
Coriander (cilantro) leaves	1 sprig, chopped
Spring onion (scallion)	1, chopped
Ulam greens (*see* Note)	150 g

Method

- Season beef with salt and pepper. Heat oil in a wok and fry beef over high heat. Set aside.
- In the same wok, sweat onions, then add chilli bean sauce and oyster sauce.
- Cook for 2 minutes before adding remaining ingredients, except *ulam* greens.
- Serve beef with *ulam* greens and spoon dressing over.

Note

The Malay word, *ulam*, refers to fresh local vegetables. It consists of various herbal leaves and garden greens chosen according to the cook's or chef's preference.

SOUPS

Cappuccino of Green Pea with
Seared Scallop and Ham and Pea Salad

Ingredients

Fresh milk	60 ml
Cream	60 ml
Green peas	105 g
Salt	to taste
Ground black pepper	to taste
Olive oil	
Red onion	5 g, peeled and chopped
Ham	10 g
Scallop	1
Butter	10 g
Warm fresh milk	5 ml
Truffle oil	3 ml
Red chilli strips	
Shichimi togarashi	

Method

- Bring milk and cream to the boil, then add 100 g green peas. Allow to boil for about 3 minutes, stirring constantly.

- Transfer to a blender (food processor) and blend until smooth.

- Return to the pot and season with salt and pepper. Adjust thickness of soup by adding a little water.

- Heat a dash of olive oil and sweat onion. Toss in remaining green peas and ham. Remove and set aside.

- In another pan, heat another dash of olive oil and sear scallop over high heat.

- Before serving, reheat soup and stir in butter. Pour soup into a cup.

- Foam warm milk with a hand blender and spoon foam on soup. Drizzle truffle oil over.

- Spoon green peas and ham into a porcelain spoon and top with scallop. Serve with soup. Garnish with red chilli and *shichimi togarashi* or as desired.

Fresh Salmon and Bean Curd with
Bonito Miso Broth

Ingredients

Water	500 ml
Dried *konbu*	1 sheet, cut to fit pot
Bonito flakes	100 g
White miso paste	20 g
Bean curd	10 g
Salmon fillet	100 g
Spring onion (scallion)	5 g, julienned

Method

⊙ Bring water to the boil then remove from heat. Add *konbu*.

⊙ Put bonito flakes into stock and allow to sit for about 45 minutes. This will allow the flavour of the bonito to infuse the stock.

⊙ Strain stock and whisk in miso paste over low heat until dissolved.

⊙ Arrange bean curd in a bowl and place salmon on it. Garnish with spring onion and bonito flakes or as desired. Serve with broth.

Note

Do not boil *konbu* as this will give it a bitter taste and will make the stock cloudy.

Roast Duck Broth with **Duck Liver** **Dumplings** and Baby Spinach

Ingredients

Roast duck	1
Water	1 litre
Duck liver	60 g, chopped
Spring onions (scallions)	20 g, chopped
Red onions	30 g, peeled and chopped
Salt	to taste
Ground black pepper	to taste
Wonton skins	18, round
Baby spinach	120 g

Method

⊚ Debone duck and boil bones in water for about 1 hour 30 minutes. Skim off any fat that surfaces in stock.

⊚ Chop duck meat and mix with duck liver, spring onions and onions. Season to taste with salt and pepper.

⊚ Divide filling evenly into 18 portions and wrap in wonton skins.

⊚ Poach dumplings for 5 minutes before serving.

⊚ Arrange spinach on a plate then place dumplings on top. Spoon broth over and serve immediately.

Note

For more flavourful dumplings, mix in some duck skin or fat when preparing the filling. This will also help to keep the dumplings moist.

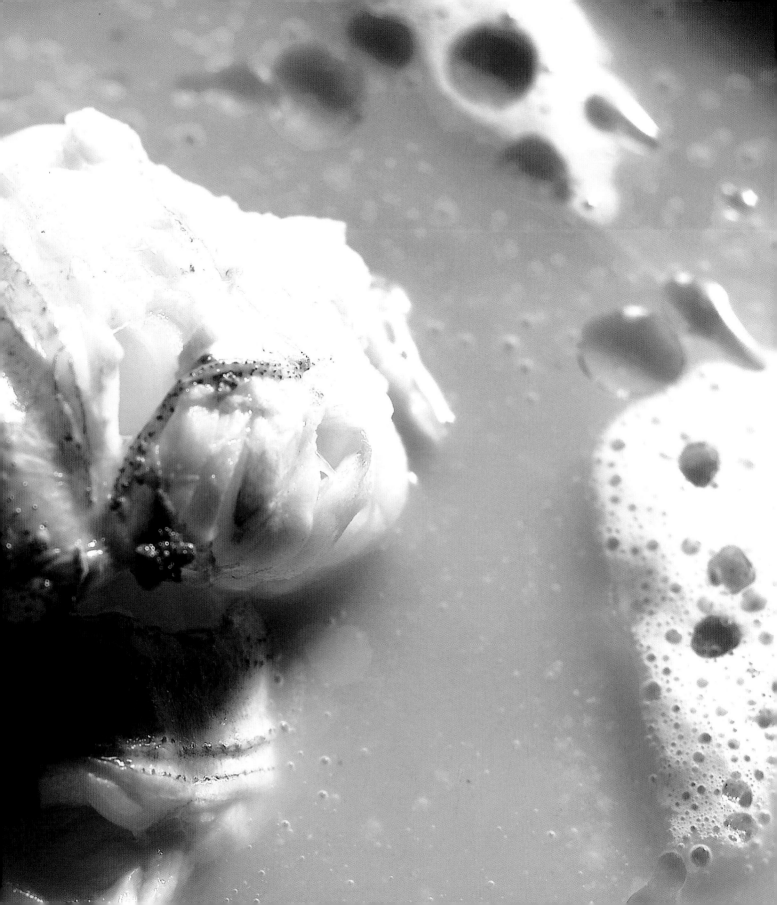

Roasted Pumpkin Soup with
Sautéed Slipper Lobster, Milk Foam and White Truffle Oil

Ingredients

Pumpkin	1, cut in half, seeds discarded
Olive oil	10 ml
Garlic	3 cloves
Salt	to taste
Ground black pepper	to taste
Chicken stock	200 ml
Slipper lobster	1, shelled
Coriander (cilantro) leaves	2 g, chopped
Warm fresh milk	5 ml
White truffle oil	2 ml

Method

- Place pumpkin on a baking tray, then drizzle with olive oil and place garlic on top. Lightly season with salt and pepper.

- Roast pumpkin in a pre-heated oven at 180°C for about 45 minutes or until pumpkin is soft.

- Scrape out flesh and blend (process) with chicken stock.

- Pour into a small soup pot and adjust the thickness by adding more chicken stock as necessary. Season to taste with salt and pepper.

- Sauté lobster with a little oil and coriander.

- Pour soup into a soup plate and add lobster.

- Foam milk with a hand blender and spoon foam on soup. Drizzle with truffle oil before serving.

Note

Every pumpkin is different. If you know your vegetable supplier well, get him to choose a really sweet one for you. The difference can be seen after you bake them. The riper ones are always sweeter.

Silk Hen Chinese Herb Broth with **Mushroom Ravioli** and Chinese Wolfberries

Ingredients

Silk hen (black chicken)	1, about 350 g
Mixed Chinese herbs for chicken soup	1 packet
Chinese wolfberries	20 g
Water	250–300 ml
Cooking oil	a dash
Red onion	5 g, peeled and chopped
Fresh shiitake mushrooms	10 g, chopped
Fresh button mushrooms	10 g, chopped
Spring onion (scallion)	2 g, chopped
Salt	to taste
Ground black pepper	to taste
Wonton skin	1, round
Coriander (cilantro) leaves	
Red chilli	

Method

⊚ Place chicken, mixed herbs and Chinese wolfberries in a pot. Add enough water to cover chicken and cook for about 1 hour 30 minutes over low, simmering heat.

⊚ Meanwhile, heat oil and sweat onion. Add mushrooms and sauté. Add spring onion and season to taste with salt and pepper.

⊚ Spoon mushrooms onto wonton skin and enclose. Poach wonton for about 3 minutes before serving. Spoon broth over and garnish with coriander and red chilli or as desired.

Note

You can purchase the mixed Chinese herbs for chicken soup from any Chinese herbal shop.

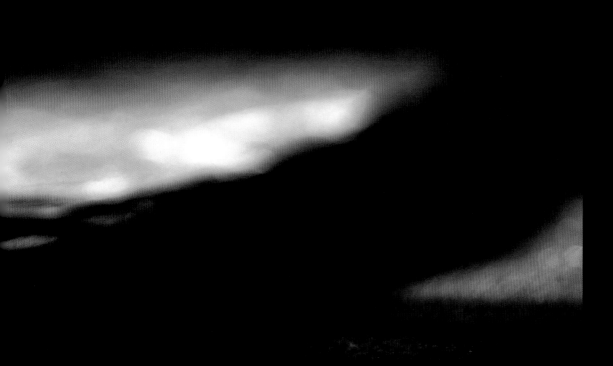

MAIN COURSES

Baked Soy Chilean Sea Bass with
Edamame Beans, Semi-dried Tomatoes and Soy Mirin Glaze

Ingredients

Chilean sea bass fillet	180 g
Japanese soy sauce	$1/2$ tsp
Mirin	1 tsp
Miso paste	$1/4$ tsp
Ground black pepper	to taste
Roma tomatoes	100 g, skinned and seeded
Rock salt	a pinch
Garlic	3 cloves, peeled and chopped
Thyme	1 sprig
Olive oil	50 ml
Edamame beans	80 g, blanched

Soy Mirin Glaze

Japanese soy sauce	50 ml
Mirin	50 ml
Sugar	20 g
Water	$1/2$ tsp
Corn flour (cornstarch)	a pinch

Method

◉ Marinate fish with Japanese soy sauce, mirin, miso and pepper for about 10 minutes before baking in a preheated oven at 180°C for about 12 minutes.

◉ Place tomatoes on a baking tray, then sprinkle with salt, garlic, thyme and olive oil. Slow roast tomatoes at 60°C until they are semi-dried. This will take about 2 hours.

◉ Prepare soy mirin glaze. Bring Japanese soy sauce, mirin, sugar and water to the boil and thicken with corn flour until the consistency of sauce is reached.

◉ Place baked fish on edamame beans and arrange tomatoes around. Drizzle with soy mirin glaze to serve.

Note

The semi-dried tomatoes can be prepared ahead of time and stored in a jar, then kept in a warm place.

Braised Lamb Shank with Oyster Sauce,
Chinese Wine and Red Dates

Ingredients

Lamb shank	1
Salt	to taste
Cooking oil	
Ground black pepper	to taste
Ginger	20 g, peeled and chopped
Garlic	5 cloves, peeled and chopped
Red onions	20 g, peeled and chopped
Red chillies	2
Chinese wine	50 ml
Oyster sauce	50 ml
Dark soy sauce	10 ml
Sesame oil	a dash
Dried red dates	5
Water	1.5 litres

Method

⊙ Season lamb shank with salt and pepper. Heat a dash of oil and sear over high heat to seal in juices. Set aside.

⊙ In a small stock pot, heat a dash of oil and sweat ginger, garlic, onions and chillies until fragrant.

⊙ Deglaze with wine, then add oyster sauce, dark soy sauce, sesame oil, red dates and water.

⊙ Allow stock to boil before adding lamb shank. Braise shank over low heat for 2 hours. Serve with vegetables of your choice.

Note

The cooked shank can kept refrigerated for up to 2 days. The flavour will improve after a day, so prepare a day in advance as desired.

Braised Pork Belly with Grilled Portobello,
Poached Egg and Pickled Ginger Mayonnaise

Ingredients

Pork belly	150 g
Cooking oil	a dash
Dark soy sauce	50 ml
Chinese wine	50 ml
Sesame oil	a dash
Water	250 ml
Portobello mushroom	1
Salt	to taste
Ground black pepper	to taste
Olive oil	a dash
Egg	1, poached

Herbs & Spices

Ginger	20 g, peeled and chopped
Red onions	20 g, peeled and chopped
Garlic	5 cloves, peeled and crushed
Cinnamon stick	1
Star anise	2
Yellow rock sugar	20 g

Pickled Ginger Mayonnaise

Pickled ginger	20 g, chopped
Mayonnaise	50 ml
Spring onions (scallions)	10 g, chopped
Lemon	1, juice extracted

Method

- Boil pork belly for about 5 minutes to remove any smell and fat.

- Heat oil and sweat herb and spices until fragrant. Add dark soy sauce, Chinese wine, sesame oil and water.

- Place pork belly in and braise for about 1 hour until pork is tender.

- Season mushroom with salt, pepper and olive oil. Grill to cook.

- Mix mayonnaise ingredients together and season to taste with salt and pepper.

- Place grilled mushroom on a plate and top with pork belly. Place poached egg on pork and spoon mayonnaise over. Sprinkle with pepper and salt and garnish as desired.

Braised Oxtail and Cépe Mushrooms
in Phyllo Pastry

Ingredients

Oxtail	480 g
Salt	to taste
Ground black pepper	to taste
Corn flour (cornstarch) for coating	
Cooking oil	
Red onions	70 g, peeled and chopped
Garlic	4 cloves, peeled and chopped
Ginger	20 g, peeled and chopped
Red chillies	2
Chinese wine	50 ml
Hoisin sauce	80 ml
Water	300 ml
Fresh cépe mushrooms	50 g, chopped
Spring onions (scallions)	20 g, chopped
Melted butter	100 ml
Phyllo pastry	3 sheets

Method

⊚ Season oxtail with salt and pepper, then coat with corn flour.

⊚ Heat a dash of oil and sear oxtail over high heat until brown. Set aside.

⊚ In another pan, heat a dash of oil and sweat 20 g onions, garlic, ginger and red chillies. Add wine and hoisin sauce followed by water.

⊚ Put oxtail in and cook over low heat for 2 hours.

⊚ Once oxtail is cooked, remove meat from bones. Heat a dash of oil and sauté meat with remaining onions, cépes and spring onions. Leave to cool.

⊚ Brush melted butter on a sheet of pastry. Spoon some meat onto pastry and wrap up like a spring roll. Repeat to make 3 rolls.

⊚ Bake in a preheated oven at 180°C for about 15 minutes until pastry is golden brown.

⊚ Serve baked pastry with braising liquid and garnish as desired.

Confit of **Miso Sake Veal Cheek** with
Asian Spice Couscous

Ingredients

Veal cheek	250 g
Miso paste	20 g
Sake	20 ml
Canola oil	300 ml
Garlic	5 cloves, peeled and chopped
Black peppercorns	10
Bay leaf	1
Thyme	1 sprig
Cooking oil	a dash
Canned chicken stock	100 ml
Couscous	100 g
Kaffir lime leaves	50 g, chopped
Basil	20 g, chopped
Lemon grass	20 g, chopped
Spring onions (scallions)	20 g, chopped
Fried shallots	20 g, peeled and chopped
Coriander (cilantro) leaves	20 g, chopped
Salt	to taste
Ground black pepper	to taste

Method

⊚ Marinate veal cheek with miso and sake for about 1 hour.

⊚ Place canola oil, garlic, peppercorns, bay leaf and thyme in a stainless steel container. Set aside.

⊚ Heat cooking oil over medium heat and sear marinated veal cheek. Once seared, transfer veal cheek to canola oil mixture.

⊚ Cover with foil and slow cook in a preheated oven at 100°C for about 2 hours.

⊚ Bring chicken stock to the boil and add couscous. Cover for about 20 minutes to cook couscous.

⊚ Use a fork to separate couscous before adding kaffir lime leaves, basil, lemon grass, spring onions, fried shallots and coriander. Season to taste with salt and pepper.

⊚ Spoon couscous onto a large plate and place veal cheek on top. Sprinkle with salt to taste before serving.

Note

It is important not to sear the veal cheek over too high heat, as the marinated meat can burn easily.

Asian **Spice Confit of Duck Leg** with
Sichuan Pepper Chilli and Salt Dust

Ingredients

Duck leg	1, about 200 g
Salt	to taste
Ground black pepper	to taste
Cooking oil	a dash
Duck fat to cover duck leg	

Spices

Star anise	2
Cinnamon stick	1
Cloves	2
Garlic	5 cloves
Black peppercorns	5
Rock salt	a pinch

Dust Powder

Sichuan peppercorns	15 berries, toasted and crushed
Flake salt	1/4 tsp
Red chilli	1, seeded and finely chopped

Method

- Season duck leg with salt and pepper. Heat oil and sear over medium heat until brown. Set aside.
- Put duck fat and spices into a small ovenproof (heatproof) pot. Put duck leg into pot and cover.
- Slow-cook duck leg in a preheated oven at 100°C for about 2 hours.
- Before serving, remove duck leg and place in a 180°C oven for about 5 minutes to make skin crispy.
- Mix dust powder ingredients together and sprinkle over duck leg. Serve with vegetables of your choice.

Note

An alternative to roasting the duck leg in the oven for a crisp skin, is to pan-fry it.

Coriander **Crusted Rack of Lamb** with
Baby Chinese White Cabbage and Orange Hoisin Sauce

Ingredients

Rack of lamb	3, each about 360 g
Salt	to taste
Ground black pepper	to taste
Cooking oil	a dash
Coriander (cilantro) leaves	1 sprig, chopped
Coriander seeds	2 g, crushed
Baby Chinese white cabbage	3 heads, blanched

Orange Hoisin Sauce

Hoisin sauce	30 ml
Honey	5 ml
Red wine vinegar	10 ml
Tomato sauce	30 ml
Curry powder	5 g
Garlic	5 g, peeled and chopped
Red chilli	5 g, seeded and chopped
Orange	2, grated for zest and squeezed for juice

Method

◉ Season lamb with salt and pepper.

◉ Heat oil and sear lamb over high heat, then roast in a preheated oven at 200°C for about 8 minutes. Set aside.

◉ Combine sauce ingredients and warm in a saucepot. Adjust thickness by adding some water.

◉ Rub lamb with some sauce and coat with coriander and coriander seeds.

◉ Before serving, roast lamb for another 5 minutes until meat is medium rare.

◉ Serve lamb with blanched vegetables and remaining sauce.

Note

Always preheat the oven before use so that the food is roasted instead of steamed.

The orange hoisin sauce can be stored in the refrigerator for up to 3 weeks. This sauce is also ideal as a seasoning for barbecuing meats.

Dark Soy Sauce Quail with
Poached Quail's Egg and Chinese Kale

Ingredients

Dark soy sauce	100 ml
Yellow crystal sugar	30 g
Water	500 ml
Cinnamon stick	1
Star anise	3
Garlic	5 cloves, peeled and chopped
Red onions	50 g, peeled and chopped
Quail	1
Corn flour (cornstarch)	½ tsp, mixed with 1 Tbsp water
Vinegar	200 ml
Quail's eggs	2
Chinese kale	120 g, blanched

Method

- Combine dark soy sauce, sugar, 300 ml water, cinnamon, star anise, garlic and red onions in a pot and bring to the boil.

- Reduce heat and put in quail. Cook for about 10 minutes, then remove from heat.

- Immerse quail in sauce for 5 minutes, then drain and leave for 10 minutes before cutting.

- Thicken sauce with corn flour mixture and set aside.

- Simmer remaining water and vinegar and then poach eggs.

- Arrange quail, Chinese kale and poached eggs on a plate. Drizzle with thickened sauce and serve.

Five-spice Duck Breast with
Sautéed Spiced Potatoes and Sweet Plum Sauce

Ingredients

Duck breast	1, about 250 g
Five-spice powder	a pinch
Salt	to taste
Ground black pepper	to taste
Cooking oil	
Red onions	20 g, peeled and chopped
Garlic	20 g, peeled and chopped
Potatoes	120 g, peeled and diced
Mustard seeds	2 g
Turmeric powder	a pinch
Spring onions (scallions)	10 g, chopped

Sweet Plum Sauce

Plum sauce	80 ml
Mirin	40 ml
Red wine vinegar	10 ml

Method

- Season duck with five-spice powder, salt and pepper.
- Heat a dash of oil and sear duck over low heat, skin side first. This will remove excess fat from the duck.
- Transfer duck to roast in a preheated oven at 180°C for about 5 minutes until skin is crisp. Leave duck to cool before cutting.
- Sweat onions and garlic with a dash of oil. Add potatoes.
- Cook until potatoes are soft, then add mustard seeds, turmeric powder and spring onions. Season to taste with salt and pepper.
- Combine sauce ingredients.
- Spoon potatoes into the centre of a plate. Cut duck into thin slices and place on top of potatoes. Drizzle with sauce.

Note

To add even more flavour to this dish, use some of the duck fat to cook the potatoes.

Ingredients

Halibut fillet	200 g
Salt	to taste
Ground black pepper	to taste
Cooking oil	

Salad

Sweet peas	80 g, peeled and blanched
New potatoes	80 g, boiled and sliced
Red onions	30 g, peeled and sliced

Grain Mustard Dressing

White wine vinegar	50 ml
Olive oil	150 ml
Grain mustard	30 g
Sugar	to taste

Method

⊙ Season fish with salt and pepper. Heat oil and pan-fry fish over medium heat until golden brown.

⊙ Toss salad ingredients together and lightly season with salt and pepper.

⊙ Whisk dressing ingredients together and adjust to taste with salt and pepper.

⊙ Arrange fish and salad on a plate. Spoon dressing over and garnish as desired.

Pan-fried Sea Bass Fillet with
Pickled Ginger Red Wine Butter Sauce

Ingredients

Sea bass fillet	200 g
Salt	to taste
Ground black pepper	to taste
Cooking oil	a dash
Red wine	50 ml
Red onions	20 g, peeled and chopped
Cream	30 ml
Butter	100 g
Pickled ginger	20 g, chopped
Spring onions (scallions)	20 g, chopped

Method

⊚ Season fish with salt and pepper. Heat oil and pan-fry fish, skin side first over medium heat.

⊚ In another pan, simmer red wine and onions over low heat until reduced by two-thirds.

⊚ Pour in cream and bring to the boil. Once boiling, whisk in butter and add pickled ginger and spring onions.

⊚ Pour sauce over fish. Serve with vegetables of your choice.

Note

If the Chinese pickled ginger is too strong for your liking, use the Japanese version which is not as pungent.

Pan-fried Sea Bream Fillet with
Baby Bitter Gourd Salad

Ingredients

Sea bream fillet	1, about 180 g
Salt	to taste
Ground black pepper	to taste
Cooking oil	
Baby bitter gourd	150 g, sliced

Salad

Red onions	50 g, peeled and sliced
Red chillies	20 g, sliced
Green chillies	20 g, sliced
Spring onions (scallions)	20 g, sliced
Tomatoes	30 g, sliced and seeded
Mustard seeds	2 g, dry-roasted
Cumin seeds	2 g, dry-roasted
Lime juice	50 ml
Sugar	to taste

Method

- Season fish with salt and pepper. Heat a dash of oil and pan-fry fish on skin side until crisp. Set aside.

- Heat a dash of oil and deep-fry sliced bitter gourd until golden brown.

- Toss the rest of the salad ingredients together before adding deep-fried bitter gourd. Adjust to taste with salt and pepper.

- Serve fish topped with salad. Garnish with parsley or as desired.

Baked Red Mullet with Tomato Lemon Salsa

Ingredients

Red mullet fillet	240 g
Salt	to taste
Ground black pepper	to taste
Olive oil	100 ml
Garlic	2 cloves, peeled and sliced
Thyme	1 sprig
Asparagus (optional)	3 spears, boiled and cut

Tomato Lemon Salsa

Ripe tomatoes	120 g, sliced and seeded
Red onions	50 g, peeled and thinly sliced
Gherkins	30 g, sliced
Lemons	2, grated for zest and squeezed for juice
Olive oil	50 ml
Sugar	to taste

Method

- Place fish fillet on a baking tray. Season with salt, pepper, olive oil, garlic and thyme. Bake in a preheated oven at 160°C for about 10 minutes.

- Combine salsa ingredients and season to taste with salt and pepper.

- Transfer baked fish to a plate and spoon salsa over. Serve with asparagus or vegetables of your choice. Garnish as desired.

Roasted Lamb Rump with
Sautéed Japanese Mushrooms and Fermented Black Bean Sauce

Ingredients

Lamb rump	180 g
Salt	to taste
Ground black pepper	to taste
Cooking oil	
Unsalted butter	20 g
Hon shimeiji mushrooms	20 g
Nameko mushrooms	20 g
Enokitake mushrooms	20 g
Red onions	20 g, peeled and chopped
Flake salt	

Fermented Black Bean Sauce

Cooking oil	a dash
Red onions	20 g, peeled and chopped
Garlic	4 cloves, peeled and chopped
Fermented black beans	10 g, soaked, drained and chopped
Chinese wine	40 ml
Oyster sauce	30 ml
Canned chicken stock	100 ml
Salt	to taste
Ground black pepper	to taste
Sugar	to taste
Corn flour (cornstarch)	1/2 tsp, mixed with 1 Tbsp water
Spring onions (scallions)	10 g, chopped

Method

- Season lamb with salt and pepper.

- Heat a dash of oil and sear lamb over high heat, then roast in a preheated oven at 180°C for about 6 minutes for lamb to be medium rare. Slice thinly just before serving.

- Heat butter and sauté mushrooms with onions. Season to taste with salt and pepper.

- Prepare sauce. In a saucepot, heat oil and sweat onions, garlic and black beans. Deglaze with wine.

- Add oyster sauce and chicken stock, then season to taste with salt, pepper and sugar.

- Thicken with corn flour mixture and add spring onions.

- Place mushrooms on a plate and top with sliced lamb. Sprinkle with flake salt as desired and serve with sauce.

Note

Soak the fermented black beans well as they may contain sand particles. This will also help remove some of the saltiness.

Roasted Veal Tenderloin with Sautéed
Mushrooms and Curry Leaf-infused Black Pepper Sauce

Ingredients

Veal tenderloin	200 g
Salt	to taste
Ground black pepper	to taste
Cooking oil	
Butter	10 g
Fresh shiitake mushrooms	20 g, cut into 4
Fresh button mushrooms	20 g, cut into 4
Oyster mushrooms	20 g, sliced
Enokitake mushrooms	10 g
Red onions	20 g, peeled and chopped
Spring onions (scallions)	10 g, chopped

Sauce

Cooking oil	a dash
Red onions	20 g, peeled and chopped
Garlic	4 cloves, peeled and chopped
Black peppercorns	20 g, crushed
Chinese wine	20 ml
Oyster sauce	30 ml
Curry leaves	6
Chicken stock	100 ml
Corn flour (cornstarch)	1/2 tsp, mixed with 1 Tbsp water

Method

⊙ Season veal with salt and pepper.

⊙ Heat a dash of oil and sear veal over high heat. Transfer to a preheated oven to cook at 180°C for about 8 minutes for veal to be medium rare.

⊙ Sauté mushrooms with onions and spring onions and season with salt and pepper.

⊙ Prepare sauce. Heat oil and sweat onions and garlic until soft. Add black peppercorns and cook for about 2 minutes. Deglaze with wine.

⊙ Add oyster sauce and curry leaves followed by stock. Simmer for about 5 minutes, then thicken with corn flour mixture.

⊙ Serve veal with sautéed mushrooms and sauce.

Note

Be careful not to overcook the black peppercorns as they will turn bitter.

Seared Tuna Steak with Miso Mustard
Sabayon and White Radish Ginger Coulis

Ingredients

Tuna steak	180 g
Salt	to taste
Ground black pepper	to taste
Cooking oil	

Sabayon

Egg yolk	1
Lemon	1, squeezed for juice
Vegetable oil	50 ml
Miso paste	10 g
Dijon mustard	5 g

Coulis

White radish	30 g, grated
Ginger	10 g, peeled and grated
Spring onions (scallions)	10 g, sliced
Red chillies	10 g, chopped
Olive oil	2 ml

Method

⊙ Season tuna with salt and pepper.

⊙ Heat oil and sear tuna over high heat. The tuna will still be raw in the middle.

⊙ Prepare sabayon. Place egg yolk and lemon juice in a bowl and whisk over a hot water bath.

⊙ Once egg mixture thickens, add oil slowly and whisk until thickened and doubled in volume.

⊙ Remove from heat and add miso paste and mustard. Set aside.

⊙ Combine coulis ingredients and lightly season with salt and pepper.

⊙ To serve, top tuna with coulis and spoon sabayon on the side. Garnish as desired.

Note

When whisking sabayon, ensure that the heat is not too high and that the whisking is consistent. Otherwise, the egg will cook too quickly and the sauce will separate.

Slow-cooked Salmon Fillet with
Simple Fennel Salad and Goma Konbu

Ingredients

Salmon fillet	200 g
Olive oil	
Salt	to taste
Ground black pepper	to taste
Fennel	120 g, sliced thinly and soaked in ice water
Lemon	1, grated for zest and squeezed for juice
Goma konbu	30 g
Chives	

Method

- Preheat oven to 180°C.
- Rub salmon with olive oil and season to taste with salt and pepper.
- Place salmon on a baking tray and bake for about 15 minutes.
- Drain fennel and marinate with lemon juice and zest. Season to taste with salt and pepper.
- Top salmon with *konbu* and garnish with chives. Serve with fennel.

Note

Use only the freshest salmon to get the best out of this recipe.

When baking the salmon, watch for a creamy white liquid that will flow from the salmon. This is the protein from the fish and it is an indication that the salmon is cooked and ready.

Steamed **Maine Lobster** with
Wakame in Hot Garlic Oil

Ingredients

Maine lobster	1, about 500 g
Salt	to taste
Ground black pepper	to taste
Ginger	20 g, peeled and julienned
Goma wakame	40 g
Spring onions (scallions)	50 g, julienned
Coriander (cilantro) leaves	40 g
Red chillies	20 g, julienned
Light soy sauce	20 ml
Sesame oil	a dash
Garlic	5 cloves, peeled and chopped

Method

- Cut lobster into halves and season with salt and pepper. Place into a steaming basket with ginger.

- Steam lobster for about 10 minutes, then transfer to a plate. Top with wakame, spring onions, coriander and chillies.

- Pour light soy sauce over prepared lobster.

- Heat sesame oil and lightly fry garlic. Carefully pour over lobster and garnish to serve.

Steamed Threadfin Belly with
Sweet Mui Choi Crust and Sautéed Chinese Leek

Ingredients

Threadfin belly	120 g
Salt	to taste
Ground black pepper	to taste
Cooking oil	a dash
Garlic	2 cloves, peeled and crushed
Leek (Chinese)	4 stalks

Sweet *Mui Choi* Crust

Sweet pickled vegetable (*mui choi*)	30 g, chopped
Spring onions (scallions)	10 g, chopped
Ginger	5 g, chopped
Garlic	2 cloves, peeled and chopped
Red chilli	1, chopped
Oyster sauce	10 ml
Sesame oil	a dash

Method

- Season fish to taste with salt and pepper. Place on a metal steaming plate.
- Combine crust ingredients and spread on fish.
- Steam for about 8–10 minutes until fish is cooked. Set aside.
- Heat oil and sweat garlic. Add leek and stir-fry to cook. Season to taste with salt and pepper.
- Arrange leek on a plate and place fish on top. Spoon juices from steaming fish over and serve.

Note

The water in the steamer should already be boiling before placing the fish in to steam. This will ensure that the cooking process is immediate and that the fish is cooked and not stewed. The heat will also quickly sear the fish, sealing in the juices to keep the fish moist.

Stir-fried Linguini with Garlic, Chilli, Mushrooms, Spinach and Spring Onion

Ingredients

Garlic	5 cloves, peeled and thinly sliced
Red chilli	1, sliced
Olive oil	10 ml
Fresh shiitake mushrooms	30 g, sliced
Fresh button mushrooms	30 g, sliced
Baby spinach	50 g
Dried linguini	160 g, boiled according to instructions on pack until al dente
Canned chicken stock	100 ml
Salt	to taste
Ground black pepper	to taste
Spring onions (scallions)	10 g, sliced

Method

⊙ Sweat garlic and chilli in olive oil.

⊙ Add mushrooms and stir-fry, then add spinach.

⊙ Add linguini and quickly stir-fry with stock. Season to taste with salt and pepper. Add spring onions and serve.

Note

For even more flavour, use a well-seasoned wok when preparing this dish.

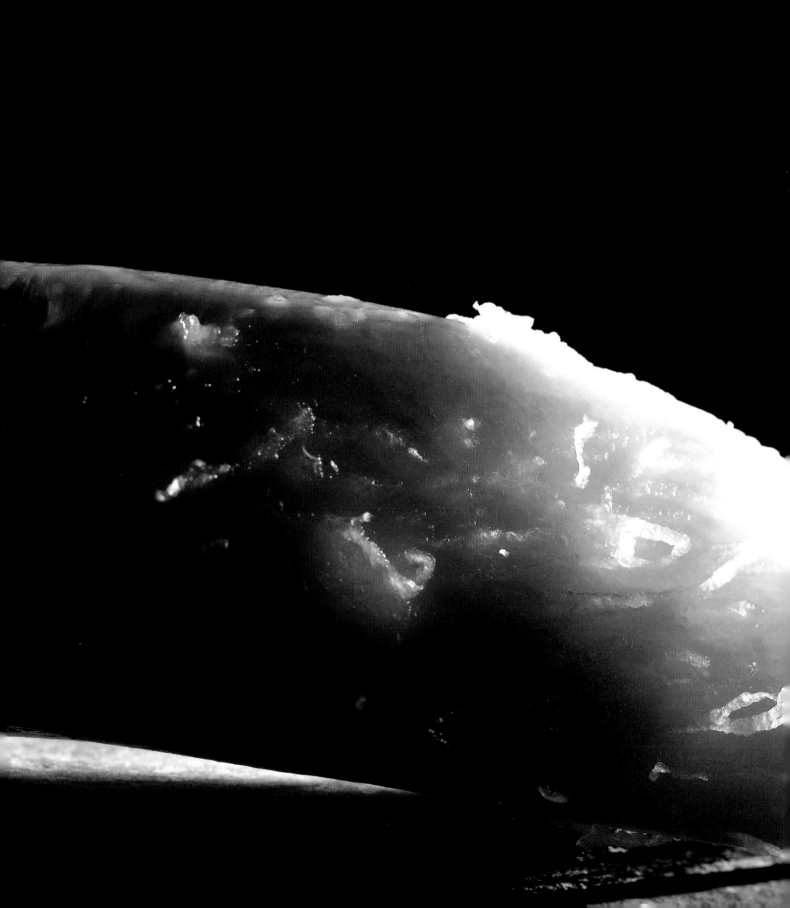

DESSERTS

Caramelised Brandy Bananas with Vanilla Ice Cream

Ingredients

Sugar	60 g
Water	10 ml
Small bananas	4, peeled
Brandy	40 ml
Almonds	20 g, toasted and chopped

Vanilla ice cream

Method

⊚ Heat sugar and water in a pan over medium heat until caramelised.

⊚ Add bananas, then deglaze with brandy.

⊚ Cook for 2 minutes, then sprinkle in almonds.

⊚ Serve with your choice of vanilla ice cream.

Note

If the sugar starts to brown too fast, add more water to stop it from burning.

Dark Muscovado **Brownie**

Ingredients

Unsalted butter	250 g
Dark chocolate	350 g
Eggs	3
Dark muscovado sugar	250 g
Plain (all-purpose) flour	60 g
Baking powder	20 g
Salt	a pinch
Almonds	150 g, chopped
Butter for greasing	
Plain (all-purpose) flour for dusting	
Icing (confectioner's) sugar for dusting	

Method

- Melt butter and chocolate in a bowl over a hot water bath.
- Whisk eggs and sugar until thick and glossy.
- Fold egg mixture into chocolate mixture and sift in flour and baking powder.
- Add salt and chopped almonds.
- Grease a 23 x 15-cm cake tin with butter and dust with flour.
- Pour mixture into cake tin and bake in a preheated oven for about 30 minutes at 180°C.
- Slice brownie and dust with icing sugar. Serve with fresh fruits, fresh cream or ice cream.

Note

To check if the brownie is ready, insert a bamboo skewer into the centre of the cake. If the skewer comes out clean, the brownie is cooked. If not, bake it a little longer.

If you are not serving it immediately, refrigerate the brownie and reheat in the microwave oven when needed.

Fresh **Mango Pancake Roll** with Mango Kulfi

Ingredients

Plain (all-purpose) flour	150 ml
Eggs	2
Milk	250 ml
Butter for greasing	
Ripe mango	1, peeled and cut into large strips
Almonds	20 g, toasted and chopped

Mango *Kulfi*

Milk	1 litre
Sugar	300 g
Canned mango purée	200 ml

Method

⊙ Make *kulfi*. Bring milk and sugar to the boil, stirring continuously, until thickened and reduced to a third. Add mango purée and freeze for about 3 hours.

⊙ Combine flour, eggs and milk to get a batter.

⊙ In a non-stick pan with a little butter, make thin pancakes.

⊙ Place a mango strip on each pancake. Sprinkle with almonds and roll pancakes up.

⊙ Serve pancake rolls with mango *kulfi*.

Note

When preparing the *kulfi*, remember to keep stirring the milk to prevent the bottom from burning.

Palm Sugar **Pudding**

Ingredients

Palm sugar	100 g
Water	100 ml
Screwpine (*pandan*) leaf	1, knotted
Eggs	2
Cream	200 ml
Mint leaves	
Assorted fresh fruit	

Method

- Heat sugar and water with screwpine leaf until sugar is dissolved. Continue to boil until syrup is thickened.

- Pour some syrup into a ramekin. Allow to cool.

- Whisk eggs and cream, then mix in remaining syrup.

- Pour egg mixture into ramekin.

- Place ramekin in a tray filled with water and bake in a preheated oven at 160°C for about 45 minutes to 1 hour.

- Remove from oven and refrigerate. Unmould pudding onto a plate and garnish with mint leaves and fresh fruit before serving.

Blackcurrant Squash Poached Pear with **Cognac Zabaglione Cream**

Ingredients

Peckham pear	1
Blackcurrant squash	300 ml
Water	100 ml

Cognac Zabaglione Cream

Egg yolks	3
Sugar	60 g
Cognac	40 ml
Whipped cream	100 ml

Method

- Peel pear and poach in blackcurrant squash and water until soft. This will take about 45 minutes.

- Prepare cream. Whisk egg yolks and sugar over a hot water bath until thickened.

- Add cognac, then fold in whipped cream.

- Put pear in a bowl with some blackcurrant poaching liquid. Spoon cream over.

Note

The poached pear can be served either warm or cold.

To test if the pear is soft enough after poaching, pierce it with a small knife. The blade should go through effortlessly.

Sago Pudding with Ching Tung

Ingredients

Sago	40 g
Dried longans	30 g
Rock sugar	80 g
Barley	20 g, boiled until cooked
White fungus	20 g, boiled until cooked
Dried persimmons	20 g, sliced
Grass jelly	20 g, julienned
Dried winter melon strips	20 g

Method

⊙ Cook sago in a pot of water. Sago is cooked when it turns translucent and floats. Drain sago and rinse in cold water. Spoon into a small ramekin.

⊙ Bring to the boil 200 ml water, dried longans and rock sugar. Leave boiling until the flavour of the longans infuses the syrup.

⊙ Add remaining ingredients and return to the boil for 2 minutes. Remove from heat and chill in the refrigerator.

⊙ Unmould sago and spoon chilled syrup and ingredients over to serve. Garnish as desired.

Simple Butter Cake with **Orange Marmalade**

Ingredients

Unsalted butter	250 g
Sugar	200 g
Eggs	5
Self-raising flour	200 g, sifted
Butter for greasing	
Plain (all-purpose) flour for dusting	
Icing (confectioner's) sugar for dusting	

Orange Marmalade

Oranges	4, cut in wedges
Water	100 ml
Sugar	200 g
Grand marnier	20 ml

Method

- Whisk butter and sugar until mixture turns light yellow and creamy.

- Add eggs one at a time, then fold in flour.

- Grease a 23 x 7.5-cm baking tin with butter and dust with flour.

- Pour batter into baking tin and bake in a preheated oven at 180°C for about 45 minutes or until cake is done.

- Prepare marmalade. Blanch orange wedges with hot water twice to remove some of the bitterness from the zest.

- Boil water and sugar, then add orange wedges and cook until mixture is dry and jam-like. Add grand marnier.

- Cut cake into slices and spoon marmalade over. Dust with icing sugar before serving.

Warm **Valrhona Chocolate** Cakes

Ingredients

Unsalted butter	250 g
Varlhona chocolate	250 g
Eggs	6
Egg yolks	6
Sugar	80 g
Plain (all-purpose) flour	40 g, sifted
Icing (confectioner's) sugar	
Ice cream	
Chopped roasted peanuts (groundnuts)	
Round aluminium moulds	12, each 6 x 4-cm
Butter for greasing	
Plain (all-purpose) flour for dusting	

Method

- Melt butter and chocolate over a hot water bath. Set aside.

- Beat eggs, egg yolks and sugar until fluffy.

- Combine egg mixture with chocolate mixture. Fold in flour.

- Grease moulds and dust with flour. Pour batter into moulds and bake in a pre-heated oven at 180°C for about 8 minutes.

- Unmould cakes and dust with icing sugar. Serve with ice cream and chopped peanuts.

Note

The batter can be prepared ahead of time and kept refrigerated in individual moulds, then baked when needed.

White Valrhona Chocolate **Panna Cotta**

Ingredients

White ivory varlhona chocolate	200 g
Cream	400 ml
Milk	200 ml
Sugar	75 g
Vanilla pod	1
Gelatine powder	30 g

Method

- Melt chocolate with cream, milk and sugar in a bowl over a hot water bath.
- Whisk until chocolate is melted and sugar is dissolved.
- Scrape vanilla seeds out and discard pod. Stir into chocolate mixture.
- Dissolve gelatine with a little warm water and stir into chocolate mixture.
- Pour mixture into 6 small moulds and allow to set in the refrigerator. Unmould and serve with fresh fruits.

Note

Vanilla essence (1 tsp) can be used in place of the vanilla pod.

GLOSSARY

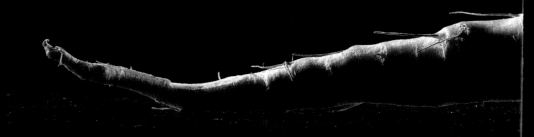

1. Baby Chinese White Cabbage

Also known as baby *bok choy*, this cabbage has a mild flavour. Both the stems and leaves are tender and are thus usually prepared whole, whether in stir-fries or in soups. Wash thoroughly before use.

2. Daikon Cress

Also known as *kaiware*, these delicate sprouts have a peppery flavour and are eaten raw, tossed in salads, or used as a garnish. Cut away the root ends before use.

3. Fennel

With a light green bulbous base, celery-like stems and feathery leaves, fennel tastes like licorice or anise and can be eaten both cooked and raw.

4. Gherkins

These small, dark green cucumbers are usually grown for pickling. They can be purchased from the supermarket, bottled in brine.

5. Leek (Chinese)

This leek comes from China and its flavour is stronger than that of western leeks. It has a thick white stalk with a bulbous end, and flat, dark green leaves that wrap around each other tightly. The leaves are usually peeled off and discarded before cooking.

6. Sweet Pickled Vegetable (Mui Choi)

This is cabbage preserved with salt and sugar. There is also another type that is simply preserved with salt. Soak well before use to remove any excess salt or sugar.

7. *Enokitake* Mushrooms

Also known as *enoki* mushrooms, these cream-coloured mushrooms have long, slender stems and small caps. They have a crisp, crunchy texture and mild taste, and can be eaten both raw or cooked. Cut away the hard base at the end of the stems and rinse briskly before use.

8. Hon Shimeji Mushrooms (White and Brown)

These small mushrooms grow in clumps on trees. They have a firm texture and aromatic peppery flavour. Cut off the hard base and rinse briskly before use.

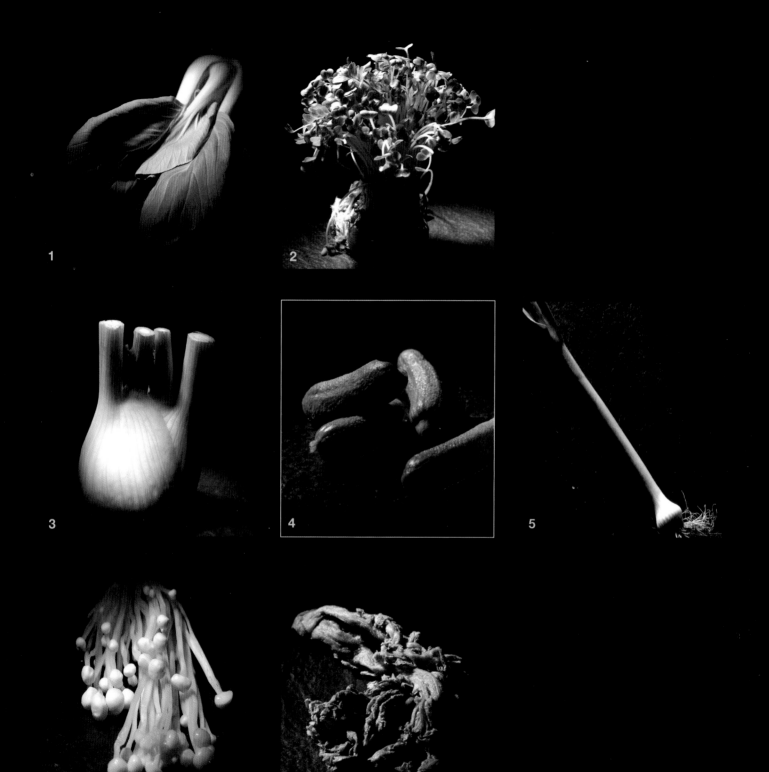

1

2

3

4

5

7

6

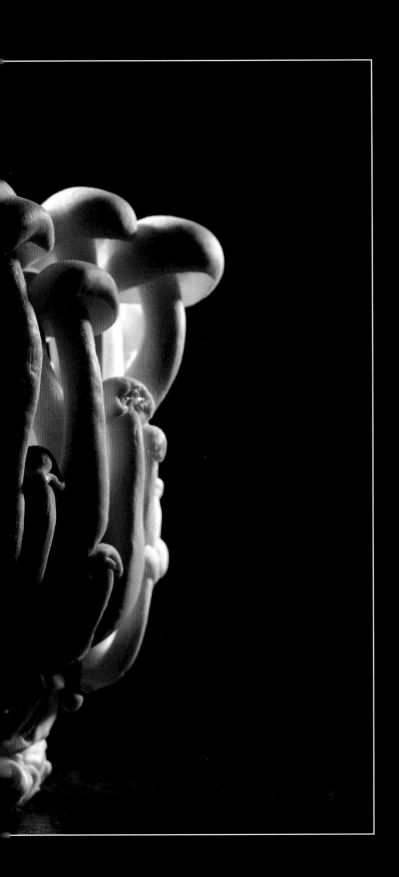

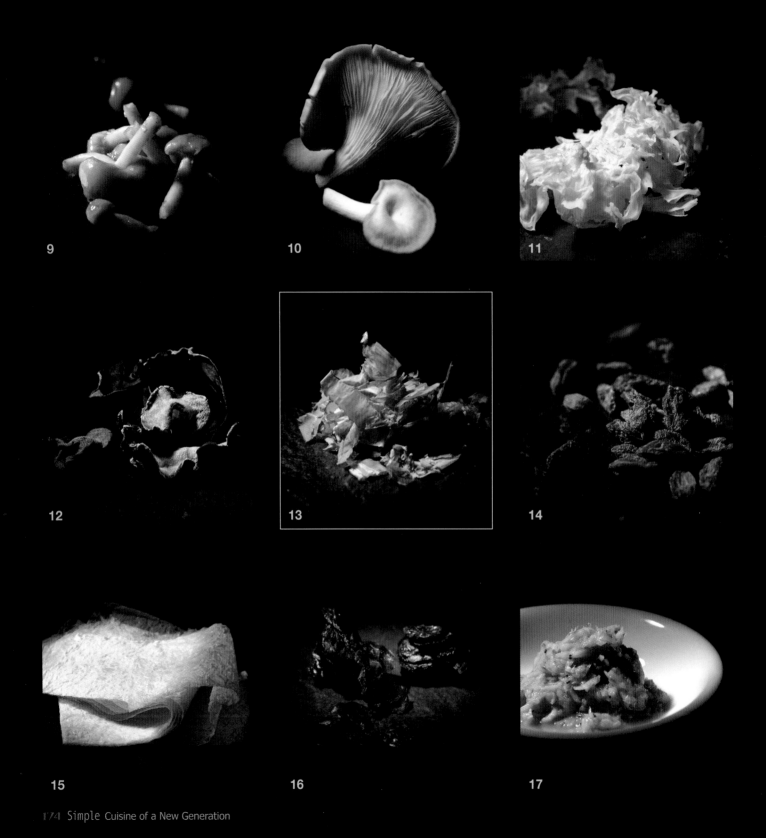

9. Nameko Mushrooms

In Japanese, nameko means 'slippery'. This probably refers to the gelatinous substance that covers the caps of the mushrooms. *Nameko* mushrooms are available only in jars or cans, preserved in brine, because of their short shelf life.

10. Oyster Mushrooms

Oyster mushrooms have flat, fan-shaped caps that vary in colour from whitish grey to brown. They have a meaty texture and are used as a meat substitute for vegetarians.

11. White Fungus

This frilly white fungus is ivory in colour and has a rounded shape. It needs to be soaked in water for at least 30 minutes to soften, after which, any hard bits should be trimmed off and discarded.

12. Wood Ear Fungus

Also known as black fungus, wood ear fungus is commonly available dried and must be reconstituted by soaking in water, just as with white fungus. It has a bland flavour that allows it to absorb the taste of the ingredients it is cooked with. It is also enjoyed for its crunchy texture.

13. Bonito Flakes

The Japanese boil, smoke, then sun-dry the tuna before flaking it to get bonito flakes. These pink paper-thin flakes are used mainly in soups, but also as garnish.

14. Chinese Wolfberries

These small red berries are usually available dried. They have a mild, sweet flavour and can be eaten raw, steeped in tea or cooked in stews and soups.

15. Dried Bean Curd Skin

This is derived from boiling soy milk and allowing a skin to form at the surface. This skin is then removed and hung to dry to get bean curd skin. Dried bean curd skin is rich in protein and can be used in both sweet and savoury preparations.

16. Dried Longans

There are two main kinds of dried longan. One comes still in the shell with the pit, and the other with just the dark, moist, sweet flesh, packed in a slab. Dried longans can be eaten as a snack or cooked in soups and desserts.

17. Fermented Prawn (Shrimp) Paste (*Cincaluk*)

This is made by fermenting fresh tiny prawns (shrimps), complete with shells, in salt. The resulting product is a thick, pink and pungent sauce. It is commonly used as a seasoning or dipping sauce in Asian cooking.

18. Dried Winter Melon Strips

These candied strips of dried winter melon make an excellent snack eaten on their own. They are also added to soups and desserts for flavour. Store in a cool dry place.

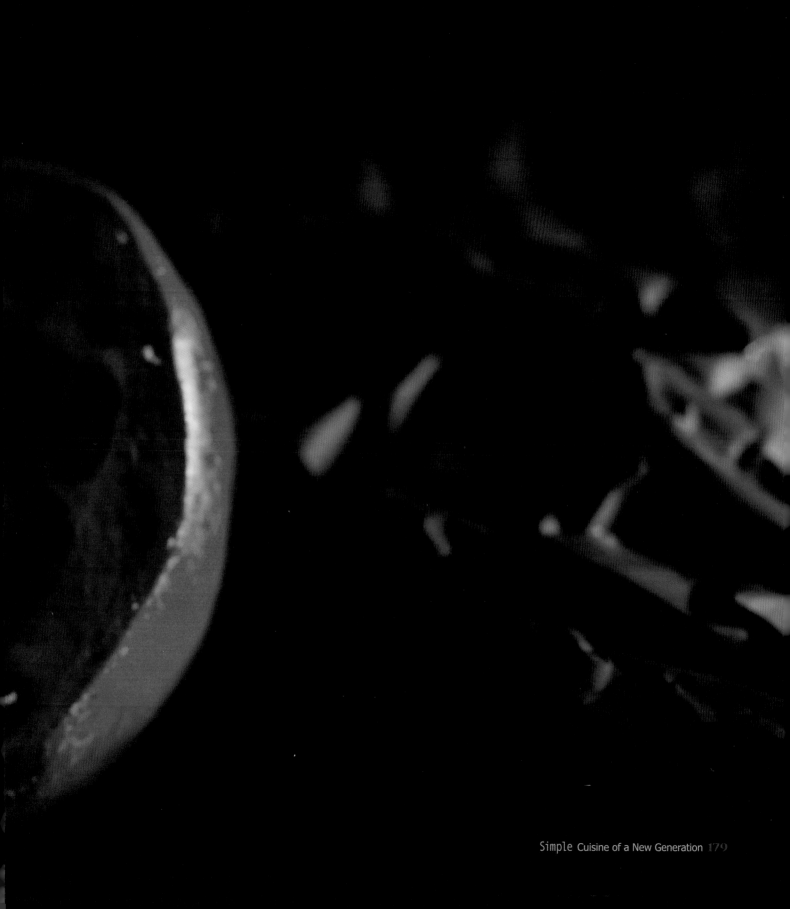

19. Flake Salt

Flake salt crystals are larger than usual table salt crystals, but the taste is delicate and mild. The crystals melt quickly and evenly compared to table salt, explaining why some chefs prefer to use it.

20. Grain Mustard

This is a grainy paste of mustard seeds, vinegar and salt. It is rather pungent but works well as a seasoning.

21. Sichuan Pepper

Despite its name, Sichuan pepper is not related to the black, white or green peppercorn family, but it is instead the berry of a rue tree. These rust coloured berries have a distinctive peppery and woody aroma. They can be used whole or crushed to add spiciness to a dish.

22. *Shichimi Togarashi*

This is a chilli mixture made from seven ground spices, including dried chillies, sesame seeds, poppy seeds and nori. It is used as a condiment or as a seasoning. It is available in small bottles in Asian supermarkets.

23. Dried *Konbu*

This dark brown or black seaweed is sun-dried and should be stored in a cool, dry place. When needed, simply wipe with a clean cloth. Do not wash, as the flavour from the natural white powder covering the *konbu* will be lost.

24. *Goma Konbu*

This is prepared kelp. The dark brown seaweed is julienned, then marinated with seasoning and sesame seeds. *Goma konbu* is available from Japanese supermarkets or gourmet stores.

25. *Goma Wakame*

Available from Japanese supermarkets or gourmet stores, this is a prepared mixture of seasoned wakame. The bright green wakame is julienned, then marinated with sesame seeds, chilli flakes, sugar and vinegar. *Goma wakame* is used as an accompaniment to dishes or as a topping.

26. Chinese Steamed Buns (*Mantou*)

Made with a mixture of flour, water and yeast, these plain steamed buns are eaten as snacks or with meals to mop up gravy. Ready-made frozen buns are available from the supermarket. Simply steam to heat and soften when needed.

27. Wonton Skin

Made from a mixture of flour and eggs, these thin sheets of rolled dough are available in the supermarket so you don't have to make them yourself. They are generally used as food wrappers for boiling or steaming.

28. *Tobiko* and Wasabi *Tobiko*

Tobiko is also known as flying fish roe and it is naturally orange in colour. These small salted eggs have a light briny flavour. Wasabi *tobiko* has been flavoured with wasabi powder, giving it a green colour and a sharper taste.

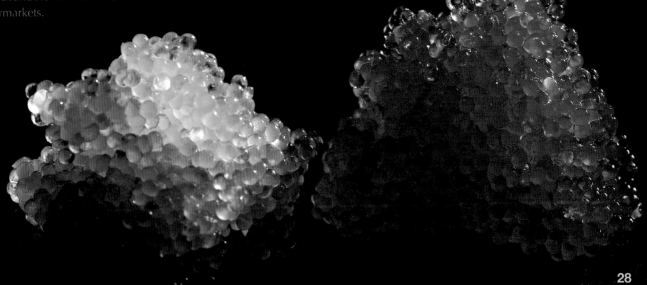

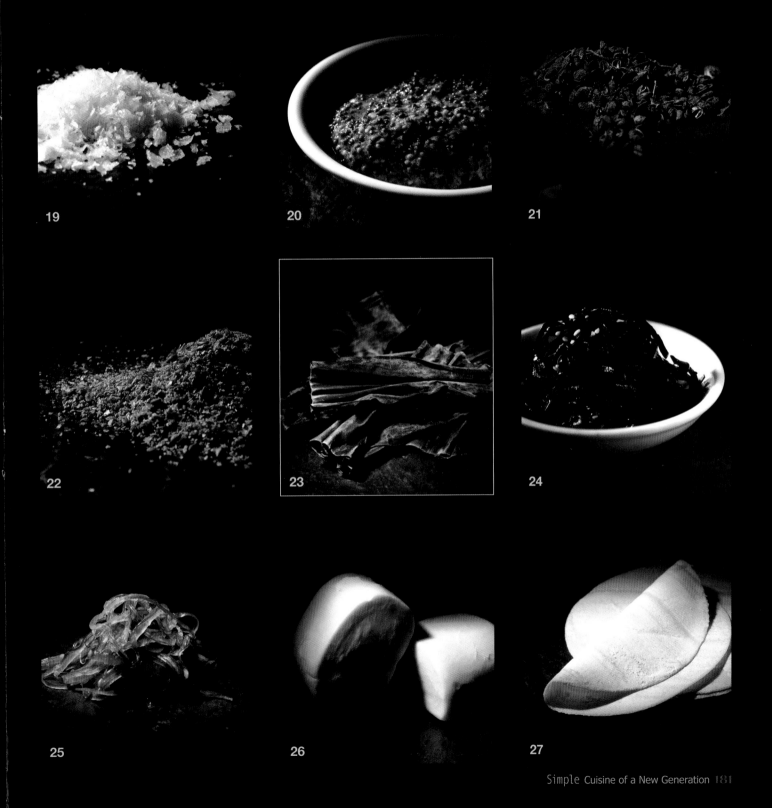

19

20

21

22

23

24

25

26

27

WEIGHTS & MEASURES

Quantities for this book are given using the metric system. Standard measurements used are:
1 tsp = 5 ml, 1 dsp = 10 ml, 1 Tbsp = 15 ml, 1 cup = 250 ml.
All measures are level unless otherwise stated.

LIQUID AND VOLUME MEASURES

Metric	Imperial	American
5 ml	1/6 fl oz	1 tsp
10 ml	1/3 fl oz	1 dsp
15 ml	1/2 fl oz	1 Tbsp
60 ml	2 fl oz	1/4 cup (4 Tbsp)
85 ml	2 1/2 fl oz	1/3 cup
90 ml	3 fl oz	3/8 cup (6 Tbsp)
125 ml	4 fl oz	1/2 cup
180 ml	6 fl oz	3/4 cup
250 ml	8 fl oz	1 cup
300 ml	10 fl oz (1/2 pint)	1 1/4 cups
375 ml	12 fl oz	1 1/2 cups
435 ml	14 fl oz	1 3/4 cups
500 ml	16 fl oz	2 cups
625 ml	20 fl oz (1 pint)	2 1/2 cups
750 ml	24 fl oz (1 1/5 pints)	3 cups
1 litre	32 fl oz (1 3/5 pints)	4 cups
1.25 litres	40 fl oz (2 pints)	5 cups
1.5 litres	48 fl oz (2 2/5 pints)	6 cups
2.5 litres	80 fl oz (4 pints)	10 cups

DRY MEASURES

Metric	Imperial
30 g	1 ounce
45 g	1 1/2 ounces
55 g	2 ounces
70 g	2 1/2 ounces
85 g	3 ounces
100 g	3 1/2 ounces
110 g	4 ounces
125 g	4 1/2 ounces
140 g	5 ounces
280 g	10 ounces
450 g	16 ounces (1 pound)
500 g	1 pound, 1 1/2 ounces
700 g	1 1/2 pounds
800 g	1 3/4 pounds
1 kg	2 pounds, 3 ounces
1.5 kg	3 pounds, 4 1/2 ounces
2 kg	4 pounds, 6 ounces

OVEN TEMPERATURE

	°C	°F	Gas Regulo
Very slow	120	250	1
Slow	150	300	2
Moderately slow	160	325	3
Moderate	180	350	4
Moderately hot	190/200	370/400	5/6
Hot	210/220	410/440	6/7
Very hot	230	450	8
Super hot	250/290	475/550	9/10

LENGTH

Metric	Imperial
0.5 cm	1/4 inch
1 cm	1/2 inch
1.5 cm	3/4 inch
2.5 cm	1 inch

ABBREVIATION

tsp	teaspoon
Tbsp	tablespoon
g	gram
kg	kilogram
ml	millilitre

Simple Cuisine of a New Generation